Learning About the Endocrine and Reproductive Systems

by Melissa L. Kim

Enslow Publishers, Inc.
40 Industrial Road
Box 398
Berkeley Heights, NJ 07922
USA

http://www.enslow.com

Dedicated to my parents, Richard and Penelope Kim,
with thanks for their everlasting support.

Acknowledgments

With thanks to: Carl Spirito, PhD, associate professor of physiology, College of Health Professions, University of New England, for providing resources and advice for this book.

Original edition published as *The Endocrine and Reproductive System* in 2003.

Library of Congress Cataloging-in-Publication Data

Kim, Melissa.
  Learning about the endocrine and reproductive systems / Melissa L. Kim.
      p. cm. — (Learning about the human body systems)
  Summary: "Learn how these two wonderful systems work together to ensure the survival of the human race and discover some amazing facts about them both"— Provided by publisher.
  Includes bibliographical references and index.
  ISBN 978-0-7660-4158-5
  1. Endocrine glands — Juvenile literature. 2. Generative organs — Juvenile literature. I. Title.
  QP187.K492 2013
  612.4 — dc23

                                        2012011101

Future editions:
Paperback ISBN: 978-1-4644-0237-1
ePUB ISBN: 978-1-4645-1155-4
PDF ISBN: 978-1-4646-1155-1

Printed in the United States of America

082012 Lake Book Manufacturing, Inc., Melrose Park, IL

10 9 8 7 6 5 4 3 2 1

To Our Readers: We have done our best to make sure all Internet addresses in this book were active and appropriate when we went to press. However, the author and the publisher have no control over and assume no liability for the material available on those Internet sites or on other Web sites they may link to. Any comments or suggestions can be sent by e-mail to comments@enslow.com or to the address on the back cover.

♻ Enslow Publishers, Inc., is committed to printing our books on recycled paper. The paper in every book contains 10% to 30% post-consumer waste (PCW). The cover board on the outside of each book contains 100% PCW. Our goal is to do our part to help young people and the environment too!

Photo Credits: © Art Explosion, Nova Development Corp., p. 24; © Corel Gallery, Corel Corp., p. 27; © Digital Stock, Corbis Corp., p. 8; John F. Kennedy Presidential Library and Museum, Boston, p. 41 (top); © Life Art, Williams & Wilkins, pp. 4, 6, 10, 11, 12, 13, 15, 17, 18, 19, 22, 26, 27, 30, 31, 39; Shutterstock.com, p.1; Vasiliki Varvaki/© 2012 Photos.com, a division of Getty Images. All rights reserved., p. 41 (bottom).

Cover Photo: Shutterstock.com

Contents

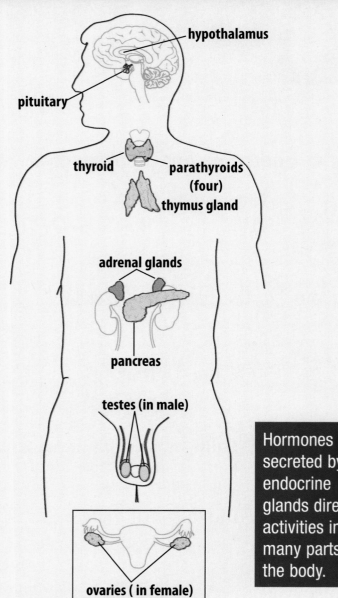

hypothalamus

pituitary

thyroid

parathyroids
(four)

thymus gland

adrenal glands

pancreas

testes (in male)

ovaries (in female)

Hormones secreted by the endocrine glands direct activities in many parts of the body.

The Endocrine and Reproductive Systems

What do a pounding heart, a beard, and a baby have in common? The endocrine system plays a key role in all three. Although it doesn't get as much attention as the reproductive system, the endocrine system is crucial. Without it, a person would never grow, would not be able to respond to change or stress, and could not turn food into energy. The endocrine system works hand in hand with the reproductive system in its role of creating babies.

The reproductive system has only one task: that of making the next generation of people. While the reproductive system plays no role in keeping an individual person alive, it is essential for the survival of the human race.

What Is an Endocrine?

There is no such thing as an endocrine. The word endocrine is an adjective. It describes something that is internal. It is almost always used to describe a **gland**. A gland is a cell or group of cells that produce and release chemicals or substances. This process is called secretion.

An **endocrine gland** is a gland that secretes substances inside the body. The substances enter the bloodstream and eventually react with cells that are in some other part of the body. The endocrine system is the network of connected endocrine glands.

There are two major types of glands, endocrine and exocrine. An **exocrine gland** is a gland that secretes substances into nearby ducts. For example, sweat is produced by exocrine glands. So is saliva.

Endocrine Glands

There are nine major glands that make up the endocrine system, ranging from the **pituitary gland** and the thyroid to the **ovaries** and the **testes**. Together, they keep the body functioning.

Some control growth and development, helping a baby grow and telling the body when to start puberty (sexual development) and

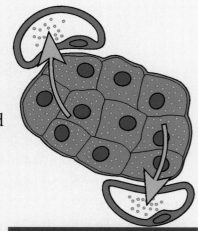

An endocrine gland secretes substances into the bloodstream.

grow body hair. Others instruct the body to convert food into energy and help to regulate the amount of sugar, salt, and water in the bloodstream.

Endocrine glands also control a woman's monthly **menstrual cycle** and the process of reproduction, or making a baby.

These glands help the body fight infection and deal with stress. When people are in physical danger, their bodies tense up, ready to confront the danger or to run away. This "fight or flight" response is possible thanks to an endocrine gland.

The Role of Hormones

Endocrine glands perform their tasks by secreting or releasing **hormones**. Hormones are chemicals that travel through the bloodstream and carry messages to organs and glands. The body has more than two hundred different hormones.[1]

Hormones tend to fall into two groups. One type, made from protein, dissolves in water. The other type is called a steroid, an organic compound that does not dissolve in water and survives longer than the protein-based hormone.

The endocrine system must carefully balance the amount of hormones in the body. Too much or too little of a hormone can be dangerous.

The endocrine glands aren't the only parts of the body that make hormones. Some organs in the body produce hormones, too. The heart produces a hormone that helps reduce blood volume and pressure. Hormones that help the body digest food are made in the stomach and intestines.

The Reproductive Cycle

Even the creation of a baby requires the endocrine glands. The sex organs, the ovaries and the testes, act as endocrine glands and are the driving forces behind the entire reproductive system. These glands, and the hormones they produce, control a woman's monthly menstrual cycle and the process of reproduction, or making a baby.

The sex organs are glands that secrete the hormones necessary to produce a baby.

Sex organs are also called the gonads. The ovaries are the female gonads, and the testes are the male gonads. Together, they secrete the hormones that are needed to produce and fertilize an egg that will grow into a baby.

The reproductive system needs these endocrine glands to function. In both men and women, reproduction is really a cycle of changes that occur in the body. The hormones produced by endocrine glands keep those cycles going. That is why it is impossible to talk about one system without the other.

Who Is on the Team?

Chapter 2

Like a baseball team, the endocrine system has nine starting players. Each one has a very different role, but they all have the same purpose: to regulate or control the body's functions.

The nine "players" are all glands. Many other parts of the body work with the endocrine system. Organs, muscles, and tissues all play a part, especially in the reproductive system.

The Pituitary Gland

The **pituitary gland** used to be thought of as the master gland. That is because the hormones it releases affect so many bodily functions. The pituitary gland makes the body grow, determines when boys and girls reach puberty (develop sexually), aids in the creation of a baby, controls how the body uses food for energy, and even makes the skin tan. About the size of a jelly bean, this gland is attached to the base of the brain.

Scientists now know that the real "master" in control of the endocrine system is found in a specific region of the brain called the **hypothalamus**. The hypothalamus, a group of nerve cells, is the part of the brain that regulates internal body processes.

A stalk of fibers attaches the pituitary gland to the hypothalamus. The hypothalamus sends messages to the pituitary gland in two ways: through nerve impulses and through chemicals in the bloodstream. In this way, the pituitary gland links the endocrine system to the nervous system.[1]

Pituitary Hormones

There are two sections, or lobes, in the pituitary gland. The hypothalamus sends instructions, through the bloodstream, to the front lobe, called the anterior lobe. There, seven important hormones are produced. Some pass along instructions to other glands, while some have a direct impact on body functions.

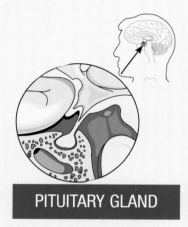

PITUITARY GLAND

Growth hormone goes into the bloodstream and affects the entire body. It determines how long the bones are, how fast a body grows, and how tall a person will be.

Pituitary hormones do many other jobs as well, including:

- Help regulate the thyroid.
- Help the body turn food into energy.
- Trigger the start of puberty. In males, they control the production of **sperm**. In females, they control the development of eggs in the ovaries.
- Turn on the production of breast milk in women who have just had a baby.

What's happening in the other part of the pituitary? The posterior lobe (in the rear of the gland) doesn't produce hormones, but it stores them. One of these hormones, made by the hypothalamus, helps the **uterus** contract when a woman gives birth. It also triggers the release of breast milk.

A second hormone works with the kidneys to control the amount of water in the body. It also helps regulate blood pressure.

Thyroid Gland

Located in the neck, the **thyroid gland** wraps around the windpipe like two wings that are connected by a narrow channel. The thyroid gland's main job is to aid the body in converting food into energy. It also helps control how fast the body uses oxygen. Growing bigger and stronger, reaching puberty, having the right heart rate and body weight—all are regulated by the thyroid gland.

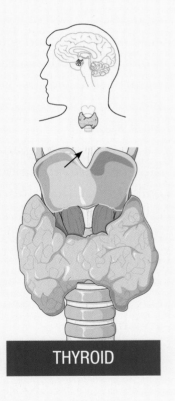

THYROID

The pituitary gland sends a message to the thyroid gland to produce and store two hormones, T3 and T4. When the thyroid gland releases these hormones into the bloodstream, they travel to the heart, liver, kidneys, and pituitary gland.

The thyroid needs iodine to create these hormones. When scientists learned this, they recommended that iodine be added to salt. Most of the salt sold in America today contains iodine. People who don't have enough iodine may develop very large thyroid glands, called goiters.

The thyroid also produces a hormone called calcitonin. This hormone, together with the **parathyroid glands**, helps regulate the amount of calcium in the bloodstream.

Parathyroid Glands

Located at the back and on each side of the thyroid gland are small pea-sized glands called the parathyroid glands. Most people have four, but some have five or even six.

These small glands maintain and regulate the amount of calcium in the blood. The body contains more calcium than any other mineral. Almost all the calcium in the body is found in the bones. The body needs calcium to keep bones strong and healthy.

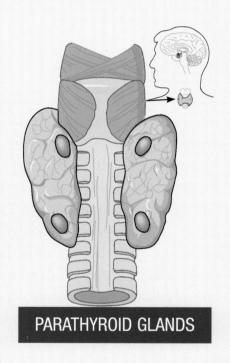

PARATHYROID GLANDS

The parathyroid glands make a hormone called the parathyroid hormone. This hormone teams up with the calcitonin made by the thyroid and with vitamin D to regulate the calcium in the body. When the parathyroid gland gets a signal from the pituitary gland, it releases its hormones to the bones, the kidneys, and the digestive system.

Adrenal Glands

The kidneys have their own pair of glands, called the **adrenal glands**. The two glands sit like a triangle-shaped hat on top of each kidney.

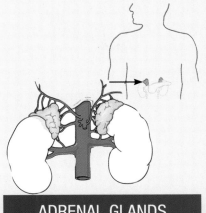

ADRENAL GLANDS

These small glands—they are less than 2 inches (5 centimeters) long—produce huge results. Hormones made by the glands can enable a woman to lift an impossibly heavy object, like a bookcase, off an injured child in an emergency. A person can run quickly to escape a vicious attack dog, thanks to these glands. The adrenal glands produce hormones that allow the body to react to stress. They help the body adapt to change, deal with injuries, and adjust to physical and emotional stress.

Because each adrenal gland is made up of two separate parts, it is really like two glands in one. The outer section is called the cortex and the inner section is called the medulla.

Like so many glands, this one gets its instructions from the pituitary gland. A pituitary hormone called adrenocorticotropic hormone (ACTH) signals the adrenal gland to make hormones. The adrenal cortex produces four main hormones, but makes thirty hormones in all. One, aldosterone, helps keep the correct level of sodium in the blood. It also maintains blood pressure and blood volume in the body.

The adrenal cortex secretes another hormone, cortisol. This substance controls the way the body uses fat, protein, and minerals. It also keeps inflammation under control. That is why cortisone, a drug made from cortisol, reduces the rash from poison ivy and eases inflamed bronchial tubes caused by asthma. The body makes a small amount of cortisol every day. If the body is attacked, it can produce up to twenty times more cortisol than normal and release it into the bloodstream.[2] This gives the body a major energy boost.

The adrenal cortex also makes two sex hormones, androgen and estrogen. Androgen is a male sex hormone, and estrogen is a female sex hormone. These hormones are produced mainly in the sex organs, but the adrenal cortex provides some of each hormone to both men and women. In women, androgen produces body hair. Scientists are not sure what role estrogen plays in a man's body.

The inner part of the adrenal gland, the medulla, sends and receives signals by nerve impulses. In times of stress, the brain sends impulses to the medulla, telling it to pump two hormones—epinephrine and norepinephrine—into the bloodstream. These hormones are also known as adrenaline (epinephrine) and noradrenaline (norepinephrine). They work with cortisol to give the body extra energy. Epinephrine makes the heart beat faster, and norepinephrine keeps blood pressure under control. A scientist first described how adrenaline worked in a 1930s study. He noticed that a cat secreted more adrenaline when a dog entered the room.

The Pancreas

The **pancreas** sits behind and below the stomach. It is about six or seven inches long. This gland is mainly an exocrine gland, producing proteins that help the body digest food. But it is also

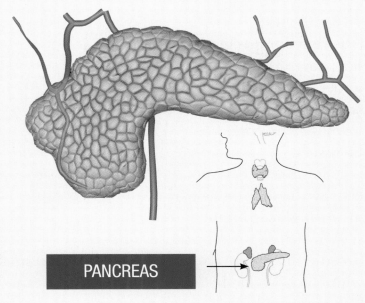

PANCREAS

an endocrine gland. Cells in a small part of the pancreas called the islets of Langerhans produce two important hormones: insulin and glucagon. Both help control the level of sugar, or glucose, in the blood. Insulin removes glucose from the blood. Glucagon increases the blood's sugar levels. The two work together to make sure the body's sugar level is balanced.

All the body's vital parts need glucose. The brain, the heart, and the muscles need glucose to work properly. The body gets most of its glucose from food, especially foods high in carbohydrates. After a person eats, levels of glucose in the blood go up. The pancreas secretes insulin, which enters the bloodstream and absorbs the glucose. This ensures that the glucose gets to the cells that need it. At the same time, the pancreas stores glucose for future use. Glucagon goes to work when levels of glucose are low. It retrieves the stored glucose and sends it into the bloodstream.

The Thymus

The tiny **thymus gland** lies above the heart, under the breastbone. It is made up of two lobes that are connected by tissues.

Some scientists classify the thymus as part of the body's immune system, the system that fights off disease. That is because the thymus produces **lymphocytes**, small white blood cells that travel in the bloodstream. The type of lymphocyte made in the thymus is called a T cell. Millions of these important cells circulate in the bloodstream. They help find and attack foreign cells that carry diseases. When T cells go into action, they divide into four types of cells. The thymus produces at least four hormones, including one called thymosin, that may help control this process.

The Pineal Gland

The **pineal gland** remains a bit of a mystery. Buried deep in the middle part of the brain, this gland is made of nerve tissue. Snakes and other reptiles have pineal cells that resemble eyes and are sensitive to light. In humans and other mammals, the pineal gland secretes a hormone called melatonin. It has been called the nighttime hormone because ten times as much melatonin is made in darkness than in light.

Scientists have known about melatonin only since the 1950s. Some think melatonin may help regulate the body's cycles of sleeping and waking. The hormone may also be linked to sexual development and breeding cycles. Studies of animals that live where winters are long and dark show that melatonin seems to delay or prevent reproduction. The animals made much melatonin in winter, when they were not sexually active. In spring, melatonin levels went down, and sexual activity increased. That may be one reason why most rabbits and birds are born in spring and summer.

The Ovaries

The ovaries are the female sex organs. Almost every female has two ovaries, one on either side of the uterus, or the womb. The **fallopian tubes** connect a woman's ovaries to her uterus.

The ovaries contain egg-forming cells called **follicle cells**. When a female is born, her ovaries contain all the follicles she will ever have. The body makes no more follicles in the course of a woman's life.

Hormones produced by the pituitary gland and by the ovaries control sexual development. When a girl reaches a certain age (which varies from person to person), these hormones trigger the beginning of puberty, the process of maturing and preparing the body to be able to have a baby.

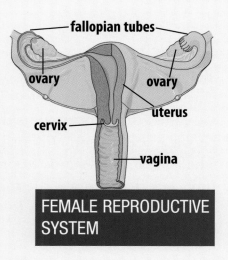

FEMALE REPRODUCTIVE SYSTEM

The pituitary gland sends messages to the ovaries causing them to produce the female sex hormone estrogen. The first time this happens marks the onset of puberty. Estrogen controls the development of breasts, nipples, and body hair, and changes in height and weight.

Hormones from the pituitary gland and the ovaries also control a woman's monthly cycle, called the menstrual cycle, which begins during puberty. During this cycle, the body grows and develops an egg and builds a lining in the uterus to receive it. If the egg is not fertilized, the egg and lining are flushed from the body and the cycle begins again.

The ovaries also produce a hormone called progesterone. This hormone prepares the uterus for pregnancy. It also makes sure the developing baby gets nutrients and helps the mother's breasts to produce milk.

A third hormone, relaxin, is also produced by the ovaries. This hormone aids in the birthing process. It helps women relax their muscles to allow a baby to pass through the birth canal.

The Testes

The testes are the male sex organs. Males have two testes, or testicles. They sit in a sac called the scrotum outside the body, between the legs on either side of the penis. The role of the testes is to produce sperm, tiny cells that contain the man's genetic information and that can fertilize eggs made by a woman.

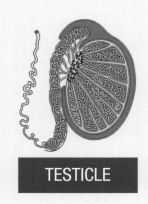

TESTICLE

18

Sperm are produced every day in tubes coiled inside the testes. In order for sperm to survive, the temperature must be three to five degrees cooler than body temperature. That is why the testes are outside the body.

Hormones produced by the testes control sexual development in males. When a boy reaches puberty, the pituitary gland sends instructions to the testes, telling them to secrete a hormone called testosterone. As the testes, scrotum, and penis grow, the testes begin to produce sperm. They produce as many as 100 million to 200 million sperm cells a day. Sperm cells are the smallest cells in the human body—all that sperm would not fill a teaspoon.

Testosterone also controls the growth of body hair. It helps determine how deep a man's voice is, how big his muscles are, and how well his body turns food into energy.

Other Members of the Team

The endocrine glands can't do all their work alone. In fact, endocrine glands would be useless without help from organs, tissues, muscles, and other parts of the body. This is especially true in the reproductive system, where the two systems work hand in hand to create babies. The endocrine system provides the "fuel" (hormones) that operates the reproductive system's "car" (ovaries and testes).

For females, the hormones produced by the ovaries control the system, but they are just one small part. Eggs form in the ovaries and then travel through one of two fallopian tubes to the uterus. The fallopian tubes are ducts that are about 4 inches (10 centimeters) long. The base or neck of the uterus is called the cervix. The cervix opens into a tube-like area called the vagina. This is the area where the male penis is placed during sexual intercourse. It also acts as the birth canal when a woman is having a baby. The baby comes out of the womb and through the vagina into the world.

For males, testosterone controls the production of sperm. But men need the services of other body parts to unite the sperm with the female's waiting egg. Once sperm are made in the testes, they travel into a tube called the epididymis, where they mature. This long coiled tube, which lies over each testicle, can measure up to 20 feet (6 meters).

The sperm then enter a duct called the vas deferens, where they can be stored for hours or days. When a man is ready to release sperm, the sperm travel from the vas deferens to another duct called the ejaculatory duct. There, sperm mix with fluids that are produced by other glands to become a thick milky fluid called semen. Semen is released, or ejaculated, from an erect penis through a narrow tube called the urethra.

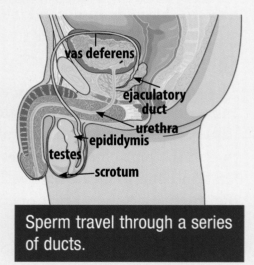

Sperm travel through a series of ducts.

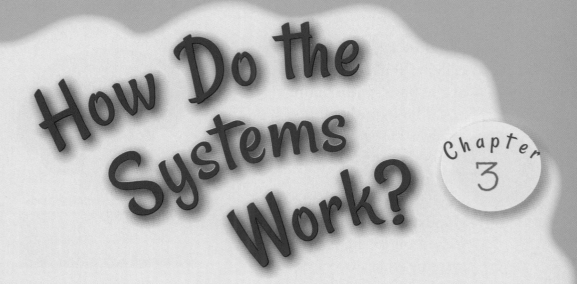

How Do the Systems Work?

Chapter 3

The endocrine and reproductive systems are complex systems that involve many parts of the body. For the systems to run smoothly, all these parts of the body need to communicate.

The Role of the Hypothalamus

It all starts in the brain. The brain receives signals from all the parts of the body. These signals inform the brain what actions need to be taken. Depending on the information in these signals, the brain starts or stops production of the hormones required to get the job done. The nervous system, using electrical and chemical signals, carries the brain's messages to the endocrine glands and the rest of the body.

The endocrine system needs to know when to release a certain hormone and how much of the substance is needed. Most of the instructions to the endocrine system come from the hypothalamus. The hypothalamus is connected to the pituitary

gland by a bundle of fibers
called a stalk. Both are located
at the base of the brain.

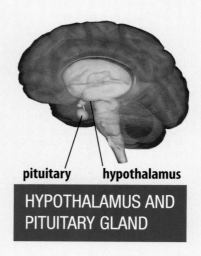

pituitary   hypothalamus

**HYPOTHALAMUS AND
PITUITARY GLAND**

The hypothalamus
receives nerve impulses from
the body's organs and tissues.
The pituitary gland also
receives messages from other
glands. This information is
passed on to the endocrine
system, which oversees the
flow of hormones.

On orders from the brain, the endocrine glands send
hormones through the bloodstream. It seems as though the
hormones must follow a difficult and random course. But
they have target cells that are looking for them.

The brain also sets the reproductive cycle in motion,
by telling the body when to start puberty. In females, the
production of hormones takes place on a monthly cycle.

Targets and Receptors

When hormones are released into the bloodstream, they are
carried along until specific target cells snatch them up. These cells,
programmed to look for specific hormones, have very sensitive
receptors on the outside of the cell. Once they spot their target,
these receptors draw the hormones in and bind them to the cell.

Most hormones—particularly those made from proteins—are
too large to enter cells. The receptor relays instructions from the
hormone to the inside of the cell. The cell then responds quickly.

The action it takes depends on the type of cell it is. For example, a gland cell may produce more of a certain chemical. A muscle cell may relax.

Some hormones, like testosterone and other steroids, are small enough to pass into the cell. They attach to receptors that are inside the cell. Then the cell responds, usually over a long period of time. Once the hormone has succeeded in making the cell carry out its function, the hormone's work is done. It may break up, and the liver, kidneys, or lungs may dissolve it. Or, it may be excreted by the kidneys and flushed from the body.

Negative Feedback

The hypothalamus acts like a central message board. If a part of the body is not working properly because a hormone level is too high, that part sends a message to the hypothalamus. In response, the hypothalamus sends messengers, usually to the pituitary gland, with instructions to make less of the hormone or to stop making it. Messages of this type—to slow or stop a process—are called negative feedback.

Positive Feedback

Sometimes the body doesn't have enough of a particular hormone. Positive feedback tells the endocrine system to produce more. Positive feedback also occurs when the production of one hormone signals the pituitary to make another hormone. For example, when estrogen in a woman's body reaches a certain level, the pituitary may begin to make more LH, luteinizing hormone, to continue the menstrual cycle.[1]

The Menstrual Cycle

Not all endocrine glands operate on a feedback loop. The sex organs have their own special cycles. The cycle followed by the female sex organs is called the menstrual cycle.

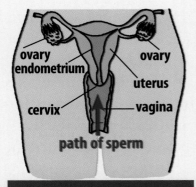

The eggs mature inside the ovaries.

When a girl reaches a certain age—which is different for each person—the hypothalamus sends signals to the pituitary gland to start producing sex hormones. This sets puberty in motion. Some girls reach puberty at nine years old, others may reach puberty at fourteen or older.

Every month, the pituitary sends follicle-stimulating hormone (FSH) to the ovaries. An egg—usually just one each month—starts to mature in one of the ovaries, in a sac called a follicle cell. Once this occurs, the follicle cell begins producing the hormone estrogen.

This signals the pituitary to make less FSH. It also signals the uterus to prepare for an egg. The uterus starts creating a lining, called the endometrium.

In mid-cycle, the pituitary increases production of LH, luteinizing hormone, and sends it to the ovaries. This prompts the follicle cell to rupture, releasing the egg into one of the fallopian tubes. The release of the egg into the fallopian tube is called ovulation.

Once the egg has been released, the remains of the follicle cell form a yellow mass called a **corpus luteum**. The corpus luteum produces progesterone and estrogen. At this point, the pituitary makes less FSH and LH, and the uterus, acting on cue from the progesterone, continues to prepare for the egg.

If a sperm does not fertilize the egg, the corpus luteum self-destructs and stops producing progesterone. This stimulates the uterus to release another hormone, prostaglandin, which shuts off the blood vessels leading to the lining. The lining of the uterus and its blood vessels break down as a result. Prostaglandin also causes the uterus to contract, forcing blood, the remains of the lining, and the unfertilized egg out of the uterus and through the vagina. This is called the menstrual flow. Too much prostaglandin can lead to cramping during the process.

The menstrual cycle varies for every female, but it usually lasts twenty-three to twenty-eight days. The amount of bleeding and the length of the bleeding period also vary from female to female. After progesterone levels have dropped and the lining has been shed, the cycle begins all over again with the production of FSH.[2]

How Reproduction Occurs

Like girls, boys begin puberty when the hypothalamus signals the pituitary gland to start producing sex hormones. Some boys reach puberty at ten years old, others may reach puberty at fourteen or even sixteen.

At puberty, FSH and LH from the boy's pituitary gland instruct the male sex organs, or testes, to make testosterone and sperm. To create a baby, these male sperm must fertilize a female egg.

To reach the egg, the sperm must travel a long journey— from a man's testes to a woman's fallopian tube. First, a man places his erect penis into a woman's vagina. Hormones carry messages from the sex organs to the man's brain and back again, causing the muscles in the testes to contract and release sperm. Fluids from other glands join the sperm to form semen.

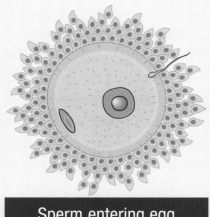

Sperm entering egg

The semen goes out through the penis and travels into and through the woman's vagina. It enters the uterus and into the two fallopian tubes. If there is an egg in one of those tubes, the sperm and the egg may join together.

Though millions of sperm are released, only a few hundred may actually make it into a fallopian tube where there is an egg. Receptors on the coating of the egg will hold the sperm. Hundreds may attach to an egg, but only one can make its way inside the egg. Once one sperm gets inside, all the others are prevented from entering. The nucleus of the sperm cell fuses with the nucleus of the egg cell and a fertilized egg is created.

The fertilized egg travels through the fallopian tube to the uterus and attaches itself to the lining of the uterus. The cells begin to divide and grow into an embryo, which develops quickly. In eight weeks, all the major organs will have formed in the embryo, and the heart will beat. At this stage, the embryo becomes a fetus.[3]

The fetus continues to grow. During pregnancy, a woman has high levels of the hormones progesterone and estrogen. Progesterone helps prepare the breasts to make milk, and estrogen helps the uterus to grow.

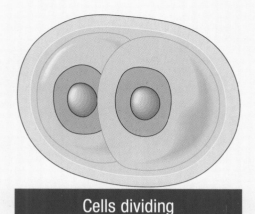

Cells dividing

After about nine months, levels of estrogen become very high in the woman's body and trigger contractions in the uterus. The hypothalamus instructs the pituitary to release the hormone oxytocin, which also causes contractions. At that point the ovaries begin secreting a hormone called relaxin, to relax the muscles in the birth canal. During the birthing process, called labor, the mother's cervix dilates, or expands, and the uterus

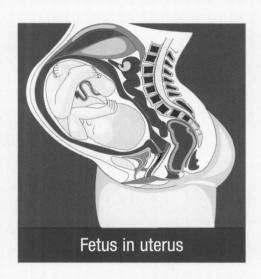

Fetus in uterus

contracts, expelling the baby through the cervix and into the outside world. A newborn baby—whose birth is so dependent on its mother's endocrine hormones—already has its own endocrine glands that are producing hormones.

Chapter 4

On the Defense

Because the endocrine and the reproductive systems are so sensitive to tiny changes in hormone levels, it doesn't take much to throw the whole operation off balance. Unfortunately, endocrine and reproductive disorders are quite common.

Too Much or Too Little

In general, problems in the endocrine system occur when the body makes either too much or too little of a hormone. When there is too much of a hormone, the condition becomes known as hyperactive. The resulting disorder usually is called by the name of the gland involved, with the prefix *hyper-* preceding it. For example, the disorder that results when a person's endocrine glands produce too much thyroid hormone is called hyperthyroidism. Too little of a hormone causes a person to have a hypoactive condition. Someone with too little thyroid hormone has hypothyroidism.

Problems in the reproductive system may also occur when there is too little or too much of a hormone. Other conditions and illnesses affect the reproductive system, too.

Common Causes

The endocrine and reproductive systems can be attacked from outside or from inside. A tumor or a cyst inside the gland is the most common cause of a hormone imbalance. Weak or damaged target and receptor cells may also cause problems. Some flaws in the endocrine system are genetic, passed from parent to child. Sometimes, scientists simply do not know the reason for a disorder.

Infections, viruses, and diseases from outside the body can attack the endocrine and the reproductive systems. Drugs, too, can have a bad effect on either or both systems. Athletes who take shots of testosterone to improve their performance can end up with serious hormonal problems, heart disease, and kidney or liver damage. People who take diet pills can damage their thyroid glands.

Diabetes

The most common endocrine system disorder is called diabetes. More than 25 million people in the United States have diabetes. Many of them may not know they have it.[1]

People with diabetes have a problem in their pancreas. The pancreas secretes insulin, which the body uses to remove glucose from the bloodstream and put it to use in other parts of the body. If the pancreas does not make enough insulin, or if the body cannot use the insulin, sugar levels in the blood become dangerously high. A person becomes very tired, feels very thirsty and hungry, needs to urinate frequently, and has cold or flu symptoms. Eventually, diabetes that goes untreated can lead to heart disease, kidney problems, nerve damage, eye disorders, and even blindness.

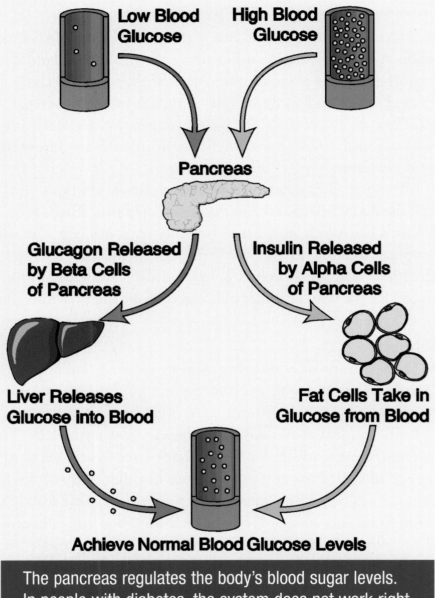

Low Blood Glucose

High Blood Glucose

Pancreas

Glucagon Released by Beta Cells of Pancreas

Insulin Released by Alpha Cells of Pancreas

Liver Releases Glucose into Blood

Fat Cells Take in Glucose from Blood

Achieve Normal Blood Glucose Levels

The pancreas regulates the body's blood sugar levels. In people with diabetes, the system does not work right.

There are two major types of diabetes. In Type I diabetes, the body makes only a small amount or no insulin. However, in Type II, the body doesn't make enough insulin or the body can't use insulin properly. Type I, the less common form, occurs most often in children. Type II, a far more common form, usually affects adults.

For people with Type I, the insulin missing from the body must be replaced. This is usually done through daily shots. Some people use a new device that attaches to the body, sending a steady supply of insulin through the bloodstream. Often people with Type II can control the condition by exercising and eating a proper diet. Some, however, have to take medication to regulate their sugar levels.

New technology has aided doctors in treating diabetes' side effects. Laser surgery can correct eye problems, a common result of long-term diabetes. Researchers are still studying the causes of Type I diabetes. Some cases are genetic. Some may be caused by a virus. Many scientists now think Type I diabetes results from a defect in the body's immune system.[2]

Thyroid Disorders

Thyroid disorders are very common. A person may not even know he or she has a mild thyroid disorder. When the

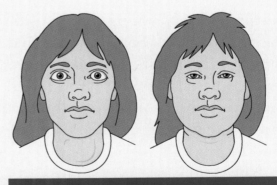

Left: Person with hyperthyroidism
Right: Person with hypothyroidism

thyroid gland makes too much or too little thyroid hormone, the gland can sometimes grow so large that it appears as a bump on the throat. This enlarged thyroid gland is called a goiter.

Hyperthyroidism or Graves' disease occurs when the thyroid gland makes too much thyroid hormone. The disease is named after a British doctor named Robert Graves, who first identified the condition in 1835.

A person with Graves' disease may have a very fast pulse, feel weak, lose weight, and be restless and irritable. The disease also causes the eyes to bulge. Doctors think a defect in the immune system may cause Graves' disease.[3] A healthy body produces antibodies, proteins created to destroy harmful cells. But in people with Graves' disease, the body produces an **antibody** that attaches itself to the thyroid cells. This antibody instructs the thyroid gland to secrete thyroid hormone. A normal thyroid secretes just enough of this hormone to keep the body healthy. But the antibody keeps telling the thyroid to make more and more of the hormone. Someone who has Graves' disease has too much hormone in the body. Graves' disease can usually be treated by taking pills with thyroid hormones that reset the balance of hormones in the body. In some cases, people may need surgery to remove part of the thyroid gland. Tumors and improper doses of diet pills may also affect the hormone balance and cause hyperthyroidism.

People with hypothyroidism don't have enough thyroid hormone. Hashimoto's disease, another immune system disorder, is one cause of hypothyroidism. Part of the body's immune system backfires and destroys cells in the thyroid gland. Hypothyroidism may be the result of surgery, for example when the thyroid is removed because of cancer or another condition. Birth defects, medications, and lack of iodine in the diet can also cause the disorder.

Like hyperthyroidism, hypothyroidism can be treated with medication. Often people with the disorder have to take pills for their lifetime to replace the missing thyroid hormone. Those who develop the disorder because of a lack of iodine can get relief by adding iodine to their diet.

Adrenal Disorders

A number of disorders affect the adrenal glands, though they are not as common as thyroid disease. In Addison's disease, the adrenal cortex doesn't make enough cortisol and aldosterone. The disorder was named for Thomas Addison, a British scientist who first described its symptoms in the mid-1800s. People with Addison's disease lose weight, have to urinate often, have low blood pressure, feel tired, and may have changes in skin color. Like Hashimoto's disease and Graves' disease, it is an immune system disorder. The body's immune system destroys cells in the adrenal cortex. Tumors, infections, or other diseases may also cause Addison's. The disorder can be treated with hormone shots.

Cushing's syndrome results when the adrenal gland makes too much cortisol. This can be caused by a tumor in the pituitary gland or by a pituitary that is not working right. The syndrome may develop if a person takes cortisol to treat arthritis or another illness. Symptoms include weak bones, obesity, a tendency to bruise easily, high blood pressure, back pain, acne, and a rounded, reddish face. Cushing's syndrome is ten times more common in women than in men.[4]

Doctors have several ways to treat the disorder. Patients can undergo radioactive treatments or chemotherapy to stop the wayward antibodies in the immune system. They can take hormone pills. Surgeons can remove one adrenal gland if a tumor in the gland is causing the syndrome. A person can live with only one adrenal gland.

Pineal Gland Disorder

Researchers suspect that a faulty pineal gland may cause a condition known as seasonal affective disorder (SAD). Those who have the disorder feel depressed, tired, and cranky. SAD usually strikes in winter, when there are fewer hours of daylight. It may be caused by an overactive pineal gland that makes too much melatonin.[5] Researchers have not yet learned why the body produces extra melatonin.

Light therapy helps some people with SAD. They sit under a high-intensity light for a while. SAD symptoms usually go away when spring comes and the days are longer.

Reproductive Problems

Cancer is one of the most common illnesses in the reproductive system. Women can have tumors in breasts, ovaries, or the uterus. Cancer can damage men's prostate or testes.

Several diseases are linked to sexual activity. Acquired Immune Deficiency Syndrome (AIDS), gonorrhea, and syphilis are some of the sexually transmitted diseases that can develop as a result of sex with an infected person.

Problems in the reproductive system can prevent a man and woman from having a child. The condition, called infertility, may be caused by problems in the man's or the woman's reproductive system, or in both. The man may produce too few sperm, or the sperm may be weak or the wrong shape. The woman may have too much or too little of a necessary hormone. She may not be ovulating because the ovaries are not producing the right amounts of estrogen and progesterone. Her fallopian tubes may be blocked.

In many cases, the problems can be treated. For example, medication may stimulate a woman's production of estrogen and progesterone. Surgery may help, as in the case of women with a painful condition called endometriosis. In this disorder, part of the uterus's lining (the endometrium) detaches and grows in other places, like the fallopian tubes. The endometrium bleeds and develops scar tissue. This may prevent ovulation or stop an egg from getting fertilized. The misplaced lining can usually be removed by surgery.

Staying Healthy

Many of the illnesses linked to the endocrine and the reproductive systems can be treated. In some cases, they can be prevented. Unfortunately, there are still no cures for most illnesses that are chronic—those that last for most of a person's life. But scientists are working hard to understand the endocrine system better. Their efforts bring new discoveries every year.

Prevention and Early Detection

The earlier a person finds the cause of a health problem, the greater the chance that doctors will be able to treat it. That is why annual check-ups are so important. Several endocrine system disorders now have tests, or screens, so that doctors can detect an illness and treat it before it gets too serious. People at high risk for Type I diabetes are among those who can be tested. Doctors use blood and urine samples to look for and track cells that interfere with insulin production in the pancreas. Type I diabetes can occur quickly and be dangerous, so it is good to know as soon as possible if the condition exists.

People who are overweight are more likely to develop Type II diabetes. They can keep the condition under control by exercising and eating a diet that is low in fat and high in fiber, whole grains, and fruits.

General good health can keep other illnesses at bay. Adrenal gland hormones help the body deal with stressful conditions. But if a person is overly stressed, too much of the stress-related hormones, adrenaline and noradrenaline, may be produced. Reducing stress, keeping blood pressure low, and eating a balanced diet can help a person stay healthy.

Alcohol and drugs can interfere with the body's endocrine and reproductive systems. For example, vasopressin, a hormone secreted in the pituitary gland, works with the kidneys to control the amount of water in the body. Alcohol prevents the body from making enough vasopressin. Drugs taken to improve athletic performance can throw off the body's hormonal balance. Athletes who take steroids can develop kidney problems, liver failure, and heart disease.

Hormone Treatments

In many cases, hormone treatments can help a person who has too little of a hormone. This is called hormone therapy or hormone replacement therapy, HRT. In the past, hormones used in treatments came from animals or people who had died. Sometimes scientists used a pancreas from a cow or pig to make insulin to treat people with diabetes. Today, scientists can make hormones in the laboratory. This advance means that people with endocrine disorders can get treatment that is safer and less expensive.

The use of HRT has become common for women who have reached menopause, the time when the ovaries stop producing estrogen. For some women, the loss of estrogen can be painful both physically and emotionally. These women can take estrogen and in some cases progesterone to help treat the hormone imbalance.

Women who have trouble getting pregnant may also use hormone therapy. Medications that contain FSH or LH, or both, help produce more than one egg in the ovaries. This increases the chance that an egg will become fertilized. Several eggs may be fertilized during the process. In those cases, the woman may have twins, triplets, or even quadruplets.

In the Future

Scientists all over the world are studying the endocrine and the reproductive systems. Major tests and studies on humans and animals will help researchers learn more about each system and identify illnesses, disorders, and treatments.

In the past few years, advances in manmade hormones have improved treatments of many endocrine and reproductive disorders. A new form of human insulin makes life much better for people with diabetes. New tools, like pumps that can be implanted into the body or controlled by a switch, make it easier for people to take insulin. Scientists are working to develop an insulin nasal spray or insulin pills.

Just as kidney and liver transplants have become more common, pancreas transplants or even transplants of the cells that make up the islets of Langerhans within the pancreas may soon be possible.

For reproductive problems, new techniques make it possible to identify exactly what and where the trouble lies. Doctors can use ultrasound, a technique that uses sound waves, to see the size and shape of the uterus and the ovaries.

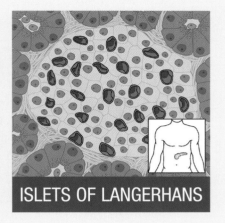

ISLETS OF LANGERHANS

A long narrow tube with a magnifying eye at one end allows a doctor to view a woman's uterus. A similar tube, inserted into a woman's abdomen, reveals a woman's fallopian tubes and ovaries. These tools help doctors see if a fallopian tube is blocked or if endometriosis exists. In some cases, they can put surgical instruments at the end of the tubes to unblock an area or operate on damaged tissue.

Techniques like these would have been hard to imagine fifty years ago. In the same way, it's hard to imagine what tools doctors will have fifty years from now. There's no doubt, however, that those tools will make life better for people with endocrine and reproductive system disorders.

Not all the research centers on disorders and their treatment, however. Many of the studies being done focus on the unsolved mysteries locked within each human body. The endocrine and the reproductive systems carry the secrets of life itself. By studying these systems, researchers hope to learn more about the creation of life and the complex workings of the human body.

Chapter 6

Amazing but True

The millions of messages that are sent to and from the brain must all pass through the hypothalamus.

The lack of only one hormone—growth hormone—causes dwarfism.

The body needs two-millionths of an ounce of salt every day.[1]

Women are eight times more likely than men to have a thyroid disorder. Four times as many women as men have seasonal affective disorder.[2]

A person can live without an adrenal medulla. A person can also live with only one adrenal gland.[3]

People used to wear "light hats," hats with light tubes under the brim, to counteract seasonal affective disorder.

At birth, a female has all the eggs she will ever have. She has one to two million at birth and about three hundred thousand at puberty. She has none left at menopause.[4]

The thymus is largest at birth. It shrinks as the body ages.[5]

Diabetes is the leading cause of blindness in adults in the United States.

The thymus may hold the key to helping people with Acquired Immune Deficiency Syndrome, or AIDS. AIDS weakens the immune system and prevents it from producing enough T cells. The hormone thymosin (made by the thymus) may be able to increase production of T cells.

President John F. Kennedy had Addison's disease. He kept it under control so well that the public never knew he had it.

Menopause, which most women experience in their fifties, may be a modern development. In 1900, women lived to be about forty-eight years old. A woman born in the United States in 2007 could expect to live to be over 80 years old.[6]

The pineal gland has existed in reptiles, mammals, and birds for millions of years. Some scientists think it may have at one time been a "third eye" in reptiles.

Chapter Notes

Chapter One: The Endocrine and Reproductive Systems

1. Brian L.G. Morgan and Roberta Morgan, *Hormones* (Los Angeles, Calif.: The Body Press, 1989), p. 21.

Chapter Two: Who Is on the Team?

1. "Pituitary Gland," *Innerbody*,. HowToMedia, Inc., <http://www.innerbody.com/text/endo03.html> (January 23, 2012)
2. Brian L.G. Morgan and Roberta Morgan, *Hormones* (Los Angeles, Calif.: The Body Press, 1989), p. 28.

Chapter Three: How Do the Systems Work?

1. Charles Clayman, M.D., ed., *The Human Body* (New York: DK Publishing Inc., 1995), p. 217.
2. Ibid.
3. Ibid., p. 201.

Chapter Four: On the Defense

1. "National Diabetes Statistics, 2011," National Diabetes Information Clearinghouse, n.d.,<http://diabetes.niddk.nih.gov/DM/PUBS/statistics> (January 24, 2012).

2. Ibid.
3. "What Is Graves Disease?", Mayo Clinic,. n.d., <http://www.mayo-clinic.com/health/graves-disease/DS00181> (January 24, 2012).
4. Brian L.G. Morgan and Roberta Morgan, *Hormones* (Los Angeles, Calif.: The Body Press, 1989), p. 134.
5. "Seasonal Affective Disorder," National Mental Health Association, n.d., <http://www.nmha.org/go/sad> (January 24, 2012).

Chapter Six: Amazing but True

1. Ramona I. Slupik, M.D., ed., *American Medical Association Complete Guide to Women's Health* (New York.: Random House, 1996), p. 624.
2. Brian L.G. Morgan and Roberta Morgan, *Hormones* (Los Angeles, Calif.: The Body Press, 1989), p. 28.
3. Karen Bellenir and Peter D. Dresser, *Diabetes Sourcebook* (Detroit, Mich.: Omnigraphics, 1995), pp. 83–90.
4. "Female Internal Genital Organs" *The Merck Manual Home Health Handbook*, n.d., <http://www.merckmanuals.com/home/womens_health_issues/biology_of_the_female_reproductive_system/female_internal_genital_organs.html> (January 24, 2012)
5. Morgan and Morgan, p. 79.
6. "Women's Health USA 2010," US Department of Health and Human Services, 2010, <http://mchb.hrsa.gov/whusa10/hstat/hi/pages/207le.html> (January 24, 2012).

Glossary

adrenal glands—Triangular glands located above each kidney. They help the body react to change and stress.

antibody—A protein produced by white blood cells that attaches to foreign organisms in the body and helps other white blood cells destroy them.

corpus luteum—Part of the female reproductive system, the follicle cell after it has released the egg. It produces the hormones estrogen and progesterone.

endocrine gland—A gland that produces or releases chemicals into the bloodstream.

exocrine gland—A gland that produces or releases chemicals into ducts.

fallopian tubes—Part of the female reproductive system, two tubes that carry eggs from the ovaries to the uterus.

follicle cells—Part of the female reproductive system; a cluster of cells in which an egg grows and develops.

gland—An organ that produces and releases a specific substance.

hormones—Chemicals secreted by an endocrine gland that carry instructions through the blood from one part of the body to another.

hypothalamus—Small cluster of cells in the brain where messages are passed between the nervous system and the endocrine system.

lymphocytes—White blood cells that travel in the bloodstream and protect the body from disease by killing foreign organisms.

menstrual cycle—A monthly cycle in women during which the body grows an egg and prepares the uterus to receive it. If the egg is not fertilized, the egg and lining are flushed from the body and the cycle begins again.

ovaries—The female sex organs. Females have one ovary on each side of the uterus where eggs develop and hormones are produced.

pancreas—A gland located behind the stomach. It works as an exocrine gland to aid in digestion and as an endocrine gland to regulate the level of glucose in the blood.

parathyroid glands—Small pea-sized glands commonly found stacked and in pairs above the thyroid gland in the neck. They maintain and regulate calcium in the bloodstream.

pineal gland—A tiny gland made up of a mass of nerve tissues located in the middle of the brain.

pituitary gland—A small gland at the base of the brain. It is also known as the master gland, because it controls other endocrine glands that in turn control body functions.

sperm—Tiny cells that contain a man's genetic information and that can fertilize eggs from a woman.

testes—The male sex organs, also called testicles, that secrete a hormone called testosterone.

thymus gland—A small gland located above the heart, under the breastbone, shaped in two lobes. It produces cells that help the immune system fight off disease.

thyroid gland—A butterfly-shaped gland in the lower part of the neck that aids in regulating the body's metabolism.

uterus—A muscular organ in a female where a fertilized egg develops into a fetus; also called the womb.

Further Reading

Books

Burnstein, John. *The Exciting Endocrine System: How Do My Glands Work?* New York: Crabtree Pub., 2009.

Cassan, Adolfo. Clark, Patrick. *Human Reproduction and Development.* Philadelphia: Chelsea House, 2006.

Klosterman, Lorrie. *Endocrine System.* New York: Marshall Cavendish Benchmark, 2009.

Olien, Rebecca. *The Endocrine System.* Mankato, Minn.: Capstone Press, 2006.

Internet Addresses

Centers for Disease Control. *BAM! Body and Mind:* Body Smartz. <http://www.bam.gov/sub_yourbody/index.html>

Nemours Foundation. Kidshealth: How the Body Works. <http://kidshealth.org/kid/>

Index